Table of Contents

INTRODUCTION 4

CHAPTER ONE 5

    What is the ketogenic diet? 5

        How does the diet work? 5

        Who is the diet suitable for? 6

        What age range is the diet suitable for? 6

        What sort of food is eaten on the diet? 6

        Classical diet 7

        Medium chain triglyceride (MCT) diet 7

        Similar dietary treatments for epilepsy 8

        Modified Atkins diet (MAD) and modified ketogenic diet 8

        Low glycaemic index treatment (LGIT) 8

        Is this a healthy way to eat? 9

        How is a person's health monitored? 9

        How is the diet monitored? 10

        Are there any side effects of the diet? 10

    Does the ketogenic diet work? 11

        How can someone start the diet? 11

    Ketogenic Diet for Epilepsy 12

        Is it effective at reducing seizures? 12

Why It Works 14

Effectiveness 15

A Typical Day's Menu 16

Eating While at School 17

CHAPTER TWO 19

Ketogenic Diet Recipes: 19

"Cornbread" Stuffing 19

'Cornbread' Muffins 21

Beef and CabbagZZZe Stir Fry 23

Beef and Chorizo Tacos with Cheesy Shells 24

Breakfast Sausage Casserole 26

Cauliflower Crust Pizza 27

Cloud Bread 30

Cranberry Sauce 31

Green Bean Casserole 33

Low Carb Mashed Potatoes 35

Mustard Cream Gravy 36

Pumpkin Cheesecake Mousse 37

Pumpkin Pie 38

Pumpkin Spice Latte 39

Strawberry Cheesecake Fat Bombs 41

Keto Chicken Parmesan 42

90-Second Keto Bread in a Mug 45

Keto Berry-Pecan Cheesecake Bars 46

Keto Coconut Lime Bars 49

Keto Cheesecake Cupcakes 53

Easy Keto Alfredo Sauce 55

Instant Pot Spicy Butternut Squash Soup 57

Best Keto Bread 58

Simple Cauliflower Keto Casserole 60

Brie Puffs 62

Keto Spaghetti Squash with Bacon and Blue Cheese
.... 64

Keto Instant Pot Soup (Low Carb) 67

Turkish Eggs (Cilbir) 69

Oven-Baked Bacon 71

One-Pan Keto Shrimp and Asparagus 73

Low-Carb Cauliflower-Spinach Side Dish 75

CONCLUSION 77

INTRODUCTION

The ketogenic diet is one treatment option for children or adults with epilepsy whose seizures are not controlled with AEDs. The diet may help to reduce the number or severity of seizures and may have other positive effects.

Up to 70% of people with epilepsy could have their seizures controlled with anti-epileptic drugs (AEDs). For some people who continue to have seizures, the ketogenic diet may help. However, the diet is very specialised. It should be carried out with the care, supervision and guidance of trained medical specialists.

It is vital that anyone using this diet for a seizure disorder do it under the supervision of an experienced physician and dietitian. Many individual variations can influence the exact diet recommendations for each person, and coordinating this eating plan with medications can be tricky. It's not something you should ever attempt on your own.

CHAPTER ONE

What is the ketogenic diet?

The ketogenic diet (KD) is a high fat, low carbohydrate, controlled protein diet that has been used since the 1920s for the treatment of epilepsy. The diet is a medical treatment and is usually only considered when at least two suitable medications have been tried and not worked.

The ketogenic diet is an established treatment option for children with hard to control epilepsy. However, adults may also benefit from dietary treatments.

Dietary treatments for epilepsy must only be followed with the support of an experienced epilepsy specialist and dietitian (food specialist).

How does the diet work?

Usually the body uses glucose (a form of sugar) from carbohydrates (found in foods like sugar, bread or pasta) for its energy source. Chemicals called ketones are made when the body uses fat for energy (this is called 'ketosis'). With the ketogenic diet, the body mostly uses ketones instead of glucose for its energy source. Research has shown that a particular fatty acid, decanoic acid, may be involved in the way the diet works.

Who is the diet suitable for?

The diet may not work for everyone but is suitable for many different seizure types and epilepsy syndromes, including myoclonic astatic epilepsy, Dravet syndrome, infantile spasms (West syndrome), and those with tuberous sclerosis. If you or your child has feeding problems, or has a condition where a high fat diet would cause problems, the diet may not be suitable.

The ketogenic diet can be adapted to all ethnic diets, as well as for people who are allergic to dairy products. The dietitian will calculate the diet and try to include foods you or your child likes.

What age range is the diet suitable for?

The diet can be used in children and adults of any age, although detailed monitoring may be needed in infants.

What sort of food is eaten on the diet?

There are different forms of the ketogenic diet. The types of foods eaten and the way each diet is calculated are slightly different, but each diet has shown effectiveness, in randomised controlled trials, in reducing seizures for some people.

Classical diet

In this diet most of the fat comes from cream, butter, oil and other naturally fatty foods. The classical diet includes very little carbohydrate and protein. Each meal includes a strictly measured ratio of fat to carbohydrate and protein.

Medium chain triglyceride (MCT) diet

MCTs are certain types of fat. This diet allows for more carbohydrates, so may offer more variety. It includes some fat from naturally fatty foods, as well as some fat from a supplement of MCT oil or emulsion. This can be mixed into food or milk and is only available on prescription.

Unlike the classical diet's strict ratio of fats to carbohydrate and protein, the MCT diet is calculated by the percentage of energy (calories) provided by these particular types of fat.

Similar dietary treatments for epilepsy

The following diets have more flexible approaches, which may suit older children or adults. They are still medical treatments, with potential side effects, and need to be approved by the person's neurologist. A ketogenic dietitian needs to individually set the diet for each person so that it is safe and nutritious.

Modified Atkins diet (MAD) and modified ketogenic diet

The Modified Atkins diet and modified ketogenic diet (sometimes called 'modified ketogenic therapy') use a high proportion of fats and a strict control of carbohydrates. These are often considered more flexible than the classical or MCT ketogenic diets, as more protein can be eaten, and approximate portion sizes may be used in place of weighed recipes.

Low glycaemic index treatment (LGIT)

This diet focuses on how carbohydrates affect the level of glucose in the blood (the glycaemic index), as well as the amount of carbohydrate eaten. Approximate portion sizes are used rather than food being weighed or measured.

Is this a healthy way to eat?

To make sure the diet is nutritionally balanced, an experienced dietitian works out exactly how much of which foods the person can eat each day. To help with this, people have individual recipes, are given support on how to plan meals, and are guided on which foods should be avoided. As the diet can be quite restrictive, the dietitian will recommend any vitamin and mineral supplements that are needed.

How is a person's health monitored?

Regular follow-ups with the dietitian, and medical team, will monitor your or your child's growth (height and weight, if applicable), health, their epilepsy, and if there is a need for any change to their anti-epileptic drugs (AEDs), such as changing to sugar-free versions. If the diet is followed carefully, individuals do not put on weight, or lose weight inappropriately.

You may be given a diary to record the number and type of seizures you or your child has while on the diet. As food can affect how we feel or act, you may be asked to note any changes in your or your child's mood, alertness and overall behaviour. It usually takes at least three months to see whether the diet is effective. The length of time the diet is followed may vary, but if an individual remains seizure-free, has fewer seizures, or maintains other benefits, such as improved quality of life, they may consider (with their medical team), slowly coming off the diet after two years.

How is the diet monitored?

To check that the diet is producing ketones, ketone levels are checked using a blood test, or a urine analysis stick, which is dipped into a container of your or your child's urine. The blood test involves a small pin prick on the finger (similar to monitoring diabetes). You can decide with your doctor which method to use.

Are there any side effects of the diet?

Constipation is common, partly due to a lack of fibre. This can be easily treated. Hunger, vomiting and lack of energy are also common at the start of the treatment, but these may decrease with time and may be avoided with careful monitoring.

Many people report an increase in energy and feeling more alert once they are used to the diet.

Does the ketogenic diet work?

A clinical trial at Great Ormond Street Hospital in 2008, and other studies since then, showed that the diet significantly reduced the number of seizures in a proportion of children whose seizures did not respond well to AEDs. After three months, around 4 in 10 (38%) children who started the diet had the number of their seizures reduced by over half, and were able to reduce their medication. Although not all children had better seizure control, some had other benefits such as increased alertness, awareness and responsiveness.

Other trials have since shown similar results in children. High quality evidence for the effectiveness of dietary treatment for adults is increasing.

Research studies are continuing to investigate how the different diets work, and why dietary treatments are effective for some people and not for others.

How can someone start the diet?

You can discuss the option of you or your child starting the diet with your GP or paediatrician/neurologist.

Ketogenic Diet for Epilepsy

Is it effective at reducing seizures?

The ketogenic diet for epilepsy (KDE) is a special diet that has helped many children and some adults achieve better (or even full) control of their seizures. It's a first-line treatment for a few specific epilepsy syndromes, such as epilepsy due to mutations in GLUT-1 or pyruvate dehydrogenase deficiency.

The ketogenic diet for epilepsy was developed in the 1920s by a Michigan doctor named Hugh Conklin. However, once effective medications were developed, the diet was used less and less frequently. It has regained recognition and has become a standard backup plan for children whose epilepsy symptoms are difficult to control with medication.1 With more than 470,000 children living with seizure disorders in the United States (according to Centers for Disease Control and Prevention statistics), it's an important addition to the arsenal of treatments for epilepsy.

Researchers are also beginning to see how it might help adults with epilepsy and people with a variety of neurologic disorders. The ketogenic diet for epilepsy is a very high-fat diet with just enough protein for body maintenance and growth, and very low amounts of carbohydrate.

When fats are broken down for energy, the body goes into what's called a ketogenic state, in which the body generates molecules called ketones. The goal of the KDE is for the brain to use ketones for energy rather than glucose (sugar) as much as possible. Ketones are (largely) water-soluble, so they are easily transported to the brain. The brain cannot use fatty acids for energy, but it can use ketones for a large portion of its energy requirements.

The KDE is usually begun in a hospital setting and often begins with a one- to two-day fasting period, though there may be a trend away from both of these requirements.

After determining the proper amount of protein (depending on age, etc.), the diet is structured as a ratio of fat grams to protein grams, plus carb grams. It usually begins with a 4 to 1 ratio and can be fine-tuned from there. The diet is often calorie and fluid-limited.4 Additionally, no packaged low-carb foods (shakes, bars, etc.) are allowed for at least the first month.

Because a gram of fat has more than twice the calories of a gram of protein or carbohydrate, this equation means that at least 75% of the calories in the diet come from fat. This is a very strict diet, and it takes time to learn how to put together meals that fit the formula. All food must be weighed and recorded.

Weaning off the diet is often attempted after two years, though some children are kept on it for longer.

Why It Works

Researchers are beginning to understand why the ketogenic diet works to lower seizure frequency. According to a 2017 review of studies, it appears that several mechanisms may be at work, including the following.

The diet appears to alter ketone metabolism in the brain in a way that enhances the brain's ability to produce the neurotransmitter GABA, which has a calming effect on the brain.[1]

The diet has significant anti-inflammatory and anti-oxidative impacts, which appear to alter the way some genes involved in epilepsy are expressed.

Certain fatty acids featured in the diet have anticonvulsant effects and have even been shown to boost the effects of valproic acid—a common anti-seizure medication.

Polyunsaturated fatty acids in the diet may prevent brain cells from becoming overexcited.

Decanoic acid, which is part of the diet as well, appears to have a direct inhibitory reaction on the AMPA receptors in the brain. These receptors are believed to play a role in epilepsy and are the target of some epilepsy medications.

Effects on a key sensor of cellular energy appear to help prevent excessive firing of brain cells.

The diet may impact circadian activities and the expression of a growth factor in the brain in a beneficial way.

Effectiveness

Studies generally show that about a third of children with epilepsy who follow the ketogenic diet will have at least a 90% reduction in seizures, and another third will experience a reduction of between 50% and 90%.46

This is remarkable, considering that these patients are generally those whose seizures are not well-controlled with medications.

A Typical Day's Menu

Below is a shortened description of a menu appearing in the 2015 Pediatric Annals article, "The Ketogenic Diet: A Practical Guide for Pediatricians." It's meant to give the idea of what children eat on the diet, not serve as an exact prescription. Remember, all of these foods are carefully weighed and measured.

Breakfast: Eggs made with heavy cream, cheese, and butter; small serving of strawberries, pineapple, or cantaloupe

Lunch: Hamburger patty topped with cheese; cooked broccoli, green beans, or carrots with melted butter; whipped heavy cream

Dinner: Grilled chicken breast with cheese and mayonnaise; cooked vegetables with butter; whipped heavy cream

Snacks: Whipped heavy cream, small servings of fruit, sugar-free gelatin

Variations substitute coconut oil or MCT oil for some of the heavy cream and butter.

Eating While at School

With a school-aged child, keeping them on the diet during the school day is difficult but essential. Thinking and planning ahead can help you be successful. You may want to try some of the following strategies:

Talk to your child: Make sure your child understands the diet and why sticking to it is essential. Let them know they shouldn't trade food with other kids. As hard as it is, they also shouldn't eat food from vending machines or treats handed out in class. Talk to the school: The teacher, guidance counselor, nurse, and administration all need to be aware of your child's special dietary needs (as well as other health-related matters). You'll want to have regular conversations with them, and you may want to have a 504 plan or individualized education plan (IEP) in place as well.

Become a planner: Gather several recipes for appropriate meals that can make convenient, easy-to-pack lunches. If possible, you may want to provide appropriate treats for your child for holiday parties and other special events that you may know about ahead of time. The Charlie Foundation and Clara's Menu are good resources for child-friendly keto recipes.

Educate family members: It's important that family members and any regular caregivers know how to prepare a meal for the child with epilepsy.

Establish routines: The timing of meals and snacks needs to be consistent in order for your child's glucose levels to remain as stable as possible. You may need to work with your child's teacher(s) on this.

Involve a friend: Having a friend at school who understands the importance of your child's diet may help them feel less awkward about being "different" and give them someone to lean on for support when needed. Make sure your child is OK with this and give them input on which friend to choose.

You'll also want to make parents of your child's friends aware of the special diet and that what some people may consider "a little harmless cheating" may not be harmless at all. It's a good idea to provide food for your child to take to parties and play dates.

CHAPTER TWO

Ketogenic Diet Recipes:

"Cornbread" Stuffing

Ingredients:

Cornbread:

- ¼ cup coconut flour
- ¼ cup almond flour
- ½ tsp. coarse salt
- ¼ tsp. baking soda
- 3 large eggs
- 1/3 cup unsweetened coconut milk (not canned)
- ½ cup coconut oil, melted

Stuffing:

- 1 Tbsp. olive oil
- ½ cup diced onion
- 1 ½ cups diced celery

- 2 cups sliced mushrooms
- 1 ½ tsp. poultry seasoning
- 1 tsp. dried sage
- 1 lb. ground sausage or bacon (review label for carb information)
- 5 cups diced "cornbread" (from above)
- 3 large eggs
- 1 ¼ cups chicken broth
- ¾ tsp. coarse salt
- ½ tsp. ground black pepper

Directions:

1. Preheat oven to 350 degrees.

2. To make cornbread: In a medium-sized bowl, mix together the dry ingredients. Slowly add the wet ingredients into the dry ingredients and stir until very smooth. Grease a small bread pan and fill about â?? of the way full with batter. Bake for 40-50 minutes or until a toothpick comes out clean. Place on a wire rack to cool. Cut into bite-sized cubes.

3. To make stuffing: Heat olive oil to medium-high heat. Add onion, celery and mushrooms and cook 3-4 minutes, until soft. Add poultry seasoning and ground sage and stir. Add sausage/bacon and cook 4-5 minutes, until browned, breaking it up into pieces with the spatula.

4. Place cornbread cubes in a large bowl and stir in sausage/bacon mixture, eggs, chicken broth and season with salt and pepper.

5. Bake 45-50 minutes, until top is browned.

Serves 12 (~1 cup per serving)

Nutrition Facts: 2.6 gm carbohydrate per serving

'Cornbread' Muffins

Jalapeno "Cornbread" Muffins

Ingredients:

- ½ cup + 1 Tbsp. almond flour

- 3 Tbsp. coconut flour
- ¼ tsp. coarse salt
- 1 tsp. baking powder
- ¼ cup coconut oil, melted
- ¼ cup powdered erythritol
- 1 large egg
- 1 large egg yolk
- ¼ cup unsweetened almond milk
- ½ cup chopped/diced jalapeno

Directions:

1. Preheat oven to 325 degrees. Grease a 12-cup muffin tin and set aside.

2. In a medium bowl, whisk together almond flour, coconut flour, salt and baking powder.

3. In a separate medium bowl, whisk together coconut oil, erythritol, egg and egg yolk until combined. Whisk in almond milk. Pour wet ingredients into the bowl of dry ingredients and use a spatula to stir just until combined. Fold in jalapeno and cheese.

4. Spoon the batter into the muffin cups and bake 20-22 minutes. Remove and allow to cool.

Makes 10 (1.5 gm carb/muffin)

Beef and CabbagZZZe Stir Fry

Ingredients:

- 2 Tbsp. grapeseed or canola oil
- 1 lb. ground chuck
- 2 cloves raw garlic, minced
- 10 oz. bag coleslaw mix
- 3 Tbsp. soy sauce
- 1 tsp. crushed red pepper flakes
- 1 tsp. rice wine vinegar
- 1 Tbsp. sesame seed oil
- ½ tsp. ground black pepper
- ¼ tsp. coarse salt
- 1 stalk green onion, sliced (optional)

Directions:

1. Heat oil in a large skillet or wok to medium-high heat. Add ground beef and cook until almost completely brown. Add garlic and coleslaw mix and saute until coleslaw is wilted, about 5-7 minutes.

2. In a small bowl, whisk together low sodium soy sauce, red pepper flakes, rice wine vinegar and sesame oil. Add the sauce to the wok and stir to combine. Season with pepper and salt.

3. Spoon mixture into bowls. Top with green onion, if desired (not included in carb count).

Serves 5

Nutrition Facts: 5.1 gm net carbs per serving

Beef and Chorizo Tacos with Cheesy Shells

Ingredients:

- 2 cups grated cheddar cheese

- ½ lb. ground beef

- ½ lb. ground chorizo

- ½ Tbsp. chili powder

- 1 medium avocado, sliced

- ¼ cup sour cream

Directions:

1. Preheat oven to 350 degrees.

2. On a baking sheet lined with parchment paper or a silicone mat, place ¼ cup cheese, 2 inches apart. Press the cheese down lightly so it makes one layer. Bake for 5-7 minutes, or until the edges of the cheese are browned. Let the cheese cool for 2-3 minutes, then lift it up and place it over the handle of a spoon or other utensil that is balanced on two cups. Let cheese cool completely, then remove.

3. While shells bake, brown beef and chorizo in a medium skillet on medium heat, stirring to break up the meat into crumbles. Stir in chili powder.

4. Scoop meat into the cheese shells and top with avocado slices and sour cream.

Serves 4

Nutrition Facts: 3.9 gm net carbs per serving

Breakfast Sausage Casserole

Ingredients:

- 10 large eggs

- 1 lb. breakfast sausage, cooked

- 1 cup of broccoli, diced and cooked

- ½ cup of freshly shredded cheddar cheese

- 6 Tbsp. sugar free syrup, divided

- ¼ cup melted butter

- 1 cup almond flour

- ¼ cup flaxseed meal

- ½ tsp. onion powder

- ½ tsp. garlic powder

- ¼ tsp. each coarse salt and ground black pepper

- ¼ tsp. dried sage

Directions:

1. Preheat the oven to 350 degrees.

2. In a large bowl, whisk eggs. Add cooked sausage, cooked broccoli, cheddar cheese, 4 tablespoons syrup and melted butter.

3. In a separate small bowl, whisk together almond flour, flaxseed meal, onion powder, garlic powder, salt, pepper and sage, until combined.

4. Slowly pour dry ingredients into wet ingredients, whisking until just combined.

5. Line a square baking pan with parchment paper. Pour mixture into the prepared pan and drizzle with remaining 2 tablespoons syrup. Bake for 45-55 minutes, until set. Allow to slightly cool and set before slicing and serving.

Serves 6-8

Net carbs: 23.3 grams per recipe; 2.9-3.9 grams per serving

Cauliflower Crust Pizza

Ingredients:

- 1 medium head cauliflower, cut into florets

- ¼ cup shredded sharp cheddar
- ¼ cup shredded mozzarella
- 1 tsp. dried Italian seasoning
- ½ tsp. coarse salt
- ½ tsp. garlic powder
- ¼ tsp. ground black pepper
- 2 large eggs

Directions:

1. Preheat oven to 425 degrees. Line a pizza pan with parchment paper and set aside.

2. Place the cauliflower florets in a food processor bowl. Process until finely crumbled (like breadcrumbs). Place cauliflower in a large glass mixing bowl. Place a paper towel on top and microwave for 3-4 minutes. Remove cauliflower and dump into a kitchen towel. Ring out all of the liquid, and then place it back into the glass bowl.

3. To the cauliflower, add the cheeses, Italian seasoning, salt, garlic, pepper and eggs. Use a spatula to stir until well combined. Press dough onto the parchment paper in a thin, even layer.

Bake for 12-15 minutes, or until browned. Remove from the oven.

4. Place topping onto the crust and smooth into an even layer. Place back in the oven and bake 7-8 minutes, until cheese is bubbly and melted.

Serves 3 (4.8 gm carb/serving)

Ideas for toppings:

- 2 Tbsp. pesto sauce (1.2 gm carb)

- 2 Tbsp. pizza sauce (2 gm carb)

- 1 cup sliced pepperoni (0 gm carb)

- 1 cup crumbled cooked sausage (0-1 gm carb - read the label)

- 2 Tbsp. black olives (1 gm carb)

- 2 Tbsp. fresh banana peppers (Less than 0.5 gm carb)

- 1 cup arugula (0.65 gm carb)

Cloud Bread

Ingredients:

- 3 large eggs, separated
- ¼ tsp. cream of tartar
- 2 oz. cream cheese, very soft
- 1 Tbsp. erythritol (if desired)

Directions:

1. Preheat oven to 350 degrees F. Line a baking sheet with parchment paper.

2. Beat egg whites and cream of tartar together until stiff peaks form.

3. Mix egg yolks, cream cheese and erythritol together in a separate, medium bowl using a wooden spoon and then hand held mixer until very smooth without visible cream cheese.

4. Gently fold egg whites into cream cheese mixture, taking care to not deflate the egg whites.

5. Carefully scoop mixture onto prepared baking sheet, forming 6 "buns".

6. Bake in preheated oven for 30 minutes, or until browned.

Serves 6

Nutrition Facts: 1.6 gm net carbohydrate per serving

Tips:

• Ensure egg whites are completely separated from the yolks. If there is any yolk, the whites will not form peaks/incorporate air.

• Buns may brown early in baking; ensure they are cooked through before removing from oven. Otherwise they might taste "eggy."

• Slice lengthwise and use as a low-carb bun for hamburgers/cheeseburgers.

Cranberry Sauce

Ingredients:

• 12 oz bag fresh cranberries

• 1 cup water

• 1 tsp unflavored gelatin powder

- ½ cup powdered erythritol

- 25 drops liquid Stevia (or to taste)

- ¼ tsp Xanthan gum dissolved in ¼ cup water (optional)

Directions:

1. Combine cranberries, water and gelatin in a saucepan. Turn heat on to medium.

2. Bring to a simmer.

3. Add the erythritol and stir until it dissolves.

4. Keep simmering until the berries pop.

5. Taste, and add liquid Stevia to adjust sweetness to your preference.

6. Remove from heat.

Optional: mix ¼ tsp xanthan gum in ¼ cup water. Use immersion blender until combined and smooth. Stir into cranberry sauce to create a more gelatinous consistency.

Makes 16 servings (2 ½ TBS each)

Nutrition Facts: 1.8 gm carbohydrate per serving

Green Bean Casserole

Ingredients:

Casserole:

- 1 lb. green beans, trimmed
- 1/3 lb. bacon (6 slices)
- ¼ cup diced onion
- 1 clove garlic, minced
- ¼ cup white wine vinegar
- 1 tsp dried parsley
- 1 tsp. lemon zest
- 6 oz. cream cheese, softened
- ½ cup cheddar cheese, shredded
- 1 tsp. Worcestershire sauce
- 1 ½ tsp Dijon mustard
- ¾ cup unsalted chicken stock
- ¾ tsp. coarse salt
- ¼ tsp. ground black pepper

Topping:

- 1/3 cup pork rinds, crushed
- 1/8 tsp. garlic powder
- 1/8 tsp. coarse salt
- 2 tsp. olive oil

Directions:

1. Preheat the oven to 375 degrees. Grease an 8x8 pan with cooking spray.

2. In a stock pot, bring 2 cups water to a boil. Add green beans, cover with a lid, and allow to cook about 10 minutes, until green beans are tender.

3. Heat skillet to medium-high. Add bacon and cook 7-8 minutes, flipping once, until crispy. Remove.

4. In the same skillet, add onion. Saute 3-4 minutes, until tender. Add garlic and saute 30-60 seconds, until fragrant. Whisk in white wine vinegar, parsley and lemon zest. Whisk in cream cheese, cheddar cheese, Worcestershire and Dijon until incorporated. Whisk in chicken stock and bring to a simmer. Allow to thicken for a few minutes. Season with salt and pepper.

5. Once green beans are cooked, stir them into the pan with the sauce. Mix to combine. Transfer to the 8x8 pan.

6. In a small bowl, stir together pork rinds, garlic powder, salt and olive. Distribute topping on the green bean mixture. Bake for 15-20 minutes, until topping is crispy.

Makes 16 servings

Nutrition Facts: 2.0 gm carbohydrate per serving

Low Carb Mashed Potatoes

Ingredients:

- 1 medium head cauliflower

- ¼ cup butter

- 2 Tbsp. sour cream

- ¼ tsp. garlic salt

- 1 pinch ground black pepper

- Chives, cheese, bacon bits, optional

Directions:

1. Bring one cup of water to simmer over medium-high heat.

2. Separate cauliflower into florets. Cook in simmering water until very tender. Drain water and add butter, sour cream, salt and ground black pepper.

3. Mash using a hand mixer, until smooth.

4. Serve with toppings of choice.

Makes 8 servings (~ ½ cup per serving)

Nutrition Facts: 2.3 gm carbohydrate per serving

Mustard Cream Gravy

Ingredients:

- 1 ½ Tbsp. Dijon mustard

- ¼ tsp. dried thyme

- ¼ cup butter

- ¼ cup heavy cream

- Pinch coarse salt and ground black pepper

Directions:

In a small saucepan, whisk together Dijon, thyme, butter, heavy cream and a pinch of salt and pepper. Bring to a simmer and cook about 10 minutes, until mixture is slightly thickened, stirring regularly.

Serves 4 (¼ cup per serving)

Nutrition Facts: 0.5 gm carbohydrate per serving

Pumpkin Cheesecake Mousse

Ingredients:

- 10 TBS pumpkin puree (100 percent pure pumpkin)
- 8 oz cream cheese, softened
- 1 tsp pumpkin pie spice
- 3 TBS heavy whipping cream
- 15 drops liquid Stevia

Directions:

1. Use an electric mixer to beat everything together until fluffy.

2. Divide into 12 dishes and chill before serving.

Makes 12 servings (2 ½ TBS each)

Nutrition Facts: 1.5 gm carbohydrate per serving

Pumpkin Pie

Ingredients:

- 15 oz can pumpkin puree (100% pure pumpkin)

- 4 oz cream cheese, softened

- 2 whole eggs, beaten

- ½ tsp pumpkin pie spice

- ½ cup heavy whipping cream

- Sugar-free sweetener equivalent to ¼ cup regular sugar

Directions:

1. Preheat oven to 350 degrees.

2. Using an electric mixer, beat pumpkin and cream cheese until smooth.

3. Beat in the eggs, pumpkin pie spice, heavy cream and sweetener.

4. Pour into greased ramekins or custard cups. Place on cookie sheet.

5. Bake for 15 minutes, or until knife inserted in center comes out clean.

Best served warm.

Makes 8 servings

Nutrition Facts: 3 gm carbohydrate per serving

Pumpkin Spice Latte

Ingredients:

- ¼ cup pumpkin puree

- 1 cup unsweetened coconut milk (not canned)

- 2 ½ Tbsp. butter

- 2 cups brewed coffee

- ½ tsp. vanilla extract

- 1 ½ Tbsp. heavy whipping cream

- 3 Tbsp. sugar-free pumpkin pie syrup

Directions:

In a medium saucepan, heat pumpkin, milk and butter over medium-low heat. Once simmering, add coffee and mix together. Remove from the stove, add vanilla extract, cream and pumpkin pie syrup. Use an immersion blender to mix. Add stevia to sweeten, if necessary.

Makes 3 servings (~1 ¼ cups per serving)

Nutrition Facts: 1.3 gm carbohydrate per serving

Strawberry Cheesecake Fat Bombs

Ingredients:

- ½ cup strawberries, washed and trimmed

- 2 Tbsp. powdered erythritol or 10-15 drops liquid stevia

- 1 tsp. vanilla extract

- ¾ cup cream cheese, softened

- ¼ cup butter, softened

Directions:

1. Place strawberries in a bowl and mash with the back of a fork, until smooth. Add the erythritol/stevia and vanilla extract and stir to mix.

2. Place the cream cheese and butter into a mixing bowl and beat with an electric mixer. Mix in the strawberry mixture until combined. Spoon into 12 small muffin molds and place in the freezer for about 2 hours.

Makes 12 (1 gm carb/bomb) or 24 (0.5 gm/ bomb)

Keto Chicken Parmesan

A delicious keto-friendly chicken Parmesan. Enjoy a classic Italian dish, and keep your macros in check!

Servings: 2

Ingredients

1 (8 ounce) skinless, boneless chicken breast

1 egg

1 table spoon heavy whipping cream

1 ½ ounces pork rinds, crushed

1 ounce grated Parmesan cheese

½ tea spoon salt

½ tea spoon garlic powder

½ tea spoon red pepper flakes (optional)

½ tea spoon ground black pepper

½ tea spoon Italian seasoning

½ cup jarred tomato sauce (such as Rao's®)

¼ cup shredded mozzarella cheese

1 tablespoon ghee (clarified butter)

Directions

Step 1

Set oven rack about 6 inches from the heat source and preheat the oven's broiler.

Step 2

Slice chicken breast through the middle horizontally from one side to within 1/2 inch of the other side. Open the two sides and spread them out like an open book. Pound chicken flat until about 1/2-inch thick.

Step 3

Beat egg and cream together in a bowl.

Step 4

Combine crushed pork rinds, Parmesan cheese, salt, garlic powder, red pepper flakes, ground black pepper, and Italian seasoning in bowl; transfer breading to a plate.

Step 5

Dip chicken into egg mixture; coat completely. Press chicken into breading; thickly coat both sides.

Step 6

Heat a skillet over medium-high heat; add ghee. Place chicken in the pan; cook until no longer pink in the center and the juices run clear, about 3 minutes per side. An instant-read thermometer inserted into the center should read at least 165 degrees F (74 degrees C). Be careful to keep breading in place.

Step 7

Transfer chicken to a baking sheet. Cover with tomato sauce; top with mozzarella cheese.

Step 8

Broil until cheese is bubbling and barely browned, about 2 minutes.

Nutrition Facts

Per Serving:

442 calories; 25.3 g total fat; 217 mg cholesterol; 1605 mg sodium. 5.8 g carbohydrates; 46.5 g protein; Full Nutrition

90-Second Keto Bread in a Mug

Ingredients

1 table spoon butter, 1/3 cup of blanched almond flour, 1 egg, 1/2 tea spoon of baking powder, 1 pinch salt

Directions

Place butter in a microwave-safe mug. Microwave until melted, about 15 seconds. Swirl mug until fully coated.

Combine almond flour, egg, baking powder, and salt in the mug; whisk until smooth.

Microwave at maximum power until set, about 90 seconds. Let cool for 2 minutes before slicing.

Nutrition Facts

Per Serving: 408 calories; 36.4 g fat; 9.8 g carbohydrates; 14.5 g protein; 194 mg cholesterol; 542 mg sodium. Full nutrition

Keto Berry-Pecan Cheesecake Bars

Ingredients

Crust:

1 cup pecans

1 tea spoon stevia-erythritol sweetener (such as Truvia®)

1 tea spoon cinnamon

¼ tea spoon ground nutmeg

2 table spoons melted butter

Filling:

1 egg

12 ounces cream cheese

½ cup stevia-erythritol sweetener (such as Truvia®)

¼ cup sour cream

½ teaspoon vanilla extract

¼ cup unsweetened almond milk

1 tablespoon melted butter

Topping:

1 cup frozen mixed berries

1 table spoon stevia-erythritol sweetener (such as Truvia®)

Directions

Step 1

Preheat the oven to 350 degrees F (175 degrees C).

Step 2

Add pecans to a food processor and chop very finely. Add sweetener, cinnamon, and nutmeg and process for a few more seconds. Pour mixture into a bowl and add melted butter. Stir together and press crust mixture into the bottom of a divided brownie pan with the divider removed.

Step 3

Beat egg until fluffy in a large bowl with an electric mixer. Mix in cream cheese 1 ounce at a time. Beat mixture until cream cheese is smooth. Add sweetener, sour cream, vanilla extract, and almond milk. Beat together until filling is smooth. Stir in melted butter. Pour filling over the crust in the brownie pan. Insert divider into the pan.

Step 4

Bake in the preheated oven for about 35 minutes.

Step 5

Meanwhile, heat a small pot over medium heat. Add mixed berries and sweetener and bring to a simmer, about 5 minutes. Stir berries and crush some with a spoon so that a liquid starts to form. Cook for about 10 minutes more.

Step 6

Allow cheesecake bars to cool in the brownie pan, about 1 hour. Pour berry sauce on top of bars.

Nutrition Facts

Per Serving:

155 calories; 14.3 g total fat; 38 mg cholesterol; 78 mg sodium. 11.2 g carbohydrates; 2.7 g protein; Full Nutrition

Keto Coconut Lime Bars

These keto lime bars are a tangy treat sure to satisfy your sweet tooth! Keep refrigerated. Garnish each piece with a small lime wedge, if desired.

Ingredients

Crust:

1 cup finely ground almond flour

¼ cup low-calorie natural sweetener (such as Swerve®)

2 table spoons of coconut flour

1 tea spoon of lime zest

¼ tea spoon of salt

3 table spoons of butter, softened

Filling:

1 cup of lime juice

½ cup of coconut milk

½ cup of low-calorie natural powdered sweetener (such as Swerve®)

1 table spoon of butter

1 tea spoon of lime zest

5 large eggs, beaten

Topping:

2 table spoons of unsweetened shredded coconut

½ table spoon of lime zest, or to taste

Directions

Step 1

Preheat the oven to 350 degrees F (175 degrees C). Grease an 8x8-inch baking dish.

Step 2

Combine almond flour, sweetener, coconut flour, lime zest, and salt in a large bowl. Mix thoroughly. Cut in butter with a fork until combined and no lumps remain. Press crust mixture down into the prepared baking dish.

Step 3

Bake in the preheated oven until lightly browned, 10 to 15 minutes. Set aside.

Step 4

Whisk lime juice, coconut milk, sweetener, butter, and zest in a medium saucepan over medium heat. Mix until sweetener is dissolved; do not let boil. Add beaten eggs slowly, a little at a time, whisking constantly until mixture is foamy and airy and starts to thicken, 5 to 10 minutes. Remove filling mixture from heat and spread evenly over the crust.

Step 5

Bake in the preheated oven until filling is set in the middle, 10 to 15 minutes.

Step 6

Toast shredded coconut in a small skillet over medium heat until lightly browned, 2 to 3 minutes. Sprinkle coconut and lime zest topping over the bars. Let cool and refrigerate completely before cutting into bars.

Cook's Notes:

The nutrition calculator doesn't factor in net carbs, so the amount of carbs listed appears higher than what is really in the bars. I used Swerve(R) as the sweetener here, and while it does contain 3 to 4 g of carbs per teaspoon, the ingredients in Swerve do not affect blood sugar, so the carbs it contains are considered non-impact. Because of this, a common practice is to subtract fiber and sugar alcohols from the carb total, making it zero carb. I have calculated the correct carbs for this recipe as 5.1g per serving, not 17.8g.

You can use granular sweetener in the filling mixture, though I prefer the powdered version since it dissolves better. You can pulse granular sweetener in a blender or food processor to achieve a powdered consistency. For a sweeter bar, add an additional 1/4 cup of sweetener to the filling mixture.

For 1 cup of lime juice, you will need approximately 8 limes.

Nutrition Facts

Per Serving:

160 calories; 13.8 g total fat; 88 mg cholesterol; 107 mg sodium. 17.8 g carbohydrates; 5.4 g protein; Full Nutrition

Keto Cheesecake Cupcakes

Very good low-carb dessert. Keto-friendly.

Ingredients

½ cup almond meal

¼ cup butter, melted

2 (8 ounce) packages cream cheese, softened

2 eggs

¾ cup granular no-calorie sucralose sweetener (such as Splenda®)

1 tea spoon vanilla extract

Directions

Step 1

Preheat oven to 350 degrees F (175 degrees C). Line 12 muffin cups with paper liners.

Step 2

Mix almond meal and butter together in a bowl; spoon into the bottoms of the paper liners and press into a flat crust.

Step 3

Beat cream cheese, eggs, sweetener, and vanilla extract together in a bowl with an electric mixer set to medium until smooth; spoon over the crust layer in the paper liners.

Step 4

Bake in the preheated oven until the cream cheese mixture is nearly set in the middle, 15 to 17 minutes.

Step 5

Let cupcakes cool at room temperature until cool enough to handle. Refrigerate 8 hours to overnight before serving.

Nutrition Facts

Per Serving:

209 calories; 20 g total fat; 82 mg cholesterol; 151 mg sodium. 3.5 g carbohydrates; 4.9 g protein; Full Nutrition

Easy Keto Alfredo Sauce

Treat yourself and guests to creamy homemade Alfredo sauce with this easy recipe. This sauce pairs well with pasta or zoodles (spiralized zucchini). You can even add chicken or shrimp. Sauce will become very thick if stored in the refrigerator. Simply heat the sauce up for it to be pourable.

Ingredients

½ cup unsalted butter

2 cloves garlic, crushed

2 cups heavy whipping cream

½ (4 ounce) package cream cheese, softened

1 ½ cups of grated Parmesan cheese

1 pinch salt, or to taste

1 pinch ground nutmeg, or to taste

1 pinch ground white pepper, or to taste

Directions

Step 1

Melt butter in a medium saucepan. Cook garlic until fragrant, about 2 minutes. Add heavy cream and cream cheese. Slowly add Parmesan cheese, stirring constantly until well incorporated and sauce thickens, 5 to 7 minutes. Stir in salt, nutmeg, and white pepper.

Per Serving:

531 calories; 53.8 g total fat; 177 mg cholesterol; 392 mg sodium. 3.8 g carbohydrates; 10.3 g protein; Full Nutrition

Instant Pot Spicy Butternut Squash Soup

Ingredients

1 table spoon of olive oil, 1 onion, diced, 2 cloves garlic, 1 pound of butternut squash - peeled, seeded, and cut into 1-inch pieces, 5 cups of vegetable broth, 1 table spoon of brown sugar, 1 tea spoon of salt, 1/2 tea spoon of ground black pepper, 1/2 tea spoon of ground ginger, 1/2 tea spoon curry powder (optional), 1 cup of heavy whipping cream.

Directions

Turn on a multi-functional pressure cooker (such as Instant Pot(R)) and select Saute function. Heat olive oil and add onion; cook until translucent, about 7 minutes. Add garlic and cook for 1 minute more.

Combine butternut squash, vegetable broth, brown sugar, salt, ground black pepper, ginger, and curry powder in the pot. Close and lock the lid. Select high pressure according to manufacturer's instructions; set timer for 10 minutes. Allow 10 to 15 minutes for pressure to build.

Release pressure carefully using the quick-release method according to manufacturer's instructions, about 5 minutes. Unlock and remove lid. Blend with an immersion blender until creamy.

Stir in heavy whipping cream.

Nutrition Facts

Per Serving: 235 calories; 17.5 g fat; 18.7 g carbohydrates; 2.7 g protein; 54 mg cholesterol; 791 mg sodium. Full nutrition

Best Keto Bread

This delicious low-carb and keto bread couldn't be any easier to make. Baked to perfection, it is ideal for slicing and making toasts or sandwiches.

Ingredients

cooking spray

7 eggs, at room temperature

½ cup of butter, melted and cooled

2 table spoons of olive oil

2 cups of blanched almond flour

1 tea spoon of baking powder

½ tea spoon xanthan gum

½ tea spoon of sea salt

Directions

Step 1

Preheat the oven to 350 degrees F (175 degrees C). Grease a silicone loaf pan with cooking spray.

Step 2

Whisk eggs in a bowl until smooth and creamy, about 3 minutes. Add melted butter and olive oil; mix until well combined.

Step 3

Combine almond flour, baking powder, xanthan gum, and salt in a separate bowl; mix well. Add gradually to the egg mixture, mixing well until a thick batter is formed.

Step 4

Pour batter into the prepared pan and smooth the top with a spatula.

Step 5

Bake in the preheated oven until a toothpick inserted into the center comes out clean, about 45 minutes.

Cook's Note:

Make sure the eggs are at room temperature; this will make the bread airy and taste better.

Nutrition Facts

Per Serving:

247 calories; 22.8 g total fat; 116 mg cholesterol; 209 mg sodium. 4.9 g carbohydrates; 7.7 g protein.

Simple Cauliflower Keto Casserole

Cauliflower in a creamy cheese sauce is a perfect keto recipe and delicious to boot! Make sure you season well with salt and pepper (nutmeg tastes great as well) otherwise it will taste too bland.

Servings: 2

Ingredients

½ head cauliflower florets

1 cup of shredded Cheddar cheese

½ cup of heavy cream

1 pinch of salt and freshly ground black pepper to taste

Directions

Step 1

Preheat the oven to 400 degrees F (200 degrees C).

Step 2

Bring a large pot of slightly salted water to a boil and cook cauliflower until tender but firm to the bite, about 10 minutes. Drain.

Step 3

Combine Cheddar cheese, cream, salt, and pepper in a large bowl. Arrange cauliflower in a casserole dish and cover with cheese mixture.

Step 4

Bake in the preheated oven until cheese is bubbly and golden brown, about 25 minutes.

Cook's Note:

Feel free to use other types of cheeses. I often use up whatever I have sitting around in the fridge.

Nutrition Facts

Per Serving:

469 calories; 40.9 g total fat; 141 mg cholesterol; 494 mg sodium. 10 g carbohydrates; 18.1 g protein; Full Nutrition

Brie Puffs

If you liked baked cheese, then you'll love this little easy-to-make snack. Low-carb and ketogenic friendly.

Servings: 1

Yield: 1 serving

Ingredients

1 ¾ ounces of Brie cheese, rind removed

1 pinch of paprika

Directions

Step 1

Line a microwave-safe plate with parchment paper.

Step 2

Cut Brie cheese into 1/2-inch cubes. Working in batches if necessary, place a few cubes onto the prepared plate, spacing them about 1 1/2 inches apart.

Step 3

Microwave on high until cheese cubes begin to puff up, 1 to 2 minutes, watching to be sure they do not burn. Cheese will appear to melt at first, but then it will puff up. Sprinkle paprika over cheese puffs and allow to cool before serving.

Nutrition Facts

Per Serving:

169 calories; 13.9 g total fat; 50 mg cholesterol; 312 mg sodium. 0.8 g carbohydrates; 10.4 g protein; Full Nutrition

Keto Spaghetti Squash with Bacon and Blue Cheese

Turn plain old spaghetti squash into a keto meal with the addition of bacon, mushrooms, spinach, and blue cheese. I like to double the blue cheese, especially when using a milder variety. Carbs in spaghetti squash can add up quickly, so use a small squash that's approximately 2 pounds.

Servings: 2 , Yield: 2 stuffed squash halves

Ingredients

1 small spaghetti squash

1 table spoon of olive oil

salt and ground black pepper to taste

4 slices bacon, cut into 1/2-inch pieces

1 (4 ounce) package mushrooms, sliced

1 clove garlic, minced

2 cups baby spinach

¼ cup sour cream

2 table spoons of crumbled blue cheese

Directions

Step 1

Preheat the oven to 400 degrees F (200 degrees C). Line a baking sheet with aluminum foil.

Step 2

Cut stem off the end of spaghetti squash using a sharp knife. Cut the squash in half lengthwise and scrape out the seeds. Brush the inside with olive oil and sprinkle with salt and pepper.

Step 3

Bake in the preheated oven until soft, about 45 minutes. Scrape cooked flesh out into a bowl and set aside. Return spaghetti squash shells to the baking sheet.

Step 4

Place bacon in a large skillet and cook over medium-high heat, turning occasionally, until evenly browned, 5 to 6 minutes. Drain bacon slices on paper towels.

Step 5

Add mushrooms and garlic to the skillet and cook for 4 to 5 minutes. Add in the cooked bacon and spinach. Stir until spinach is wilted, 2 to 3 minutes.

Add mushroom mixture to the bowl of squash. Mix in sour cream, salt, and pepper. Stir until filling is evenly combined.

Step 6

Spoon filling back into the squash shells. Sprinkle each half with 1 tablespoon blue cheese. Return to the oven and bake until cheese is melted and squash is heated through, 4 to 5 minutes.

Cook's Note:

Cutting the stem off the spaghetti squash will make halving it lengthwise much easier.

Nutrition Facts

Per Serving:

339 calories; 24.3 g total fat; 39 mg cholesterol; 691 mg sodium. 20.6 g carbohydrates; 13.5 g protein; Full Nutrition

Keto Instant Pot Soup (Low Carb)

6 servings

347 cals

Ingredients

1 table spoon of olive oil, 1 large yellow onion diced, 2 cloves of garlic minced, 1 head of cauliflower, coarsely chopped, 1 green bell pepper chopped (optional), 1 table spoon of onion powder salt and ground black pepper to taste, 1 (32 fluid ounce) container chicken stock, 2 cups of shredded Cheddar cheese, 1 cup half-and-half 6 slices of cooked turkey bacon diced, 1 table spoon Dijon mustard 4 dashes hot pepper sauce.

Directions

Turn on a multi-cooker (such as Instant Pot(R)) and select the Saute function. Add olive oil, onion, and garlic; cook until browned, about 3 minutes. Add cauliflower, green bell pepper, onion powder, salt, and pepper. Pour in chicken stock; close and lock the lid. Select Soup function; set timer for 15 minutes. Allow 10 to 15 minutes for pressure to build.

Release pressure carefully using the quick-release method according to manufacturer's instructions, about 5 minutes. Unlock and remove lid. Add Cheddar cheese, half-and-half, turkey bacon, Dijon mustard, and hot sauce. Reselect Saute function; cook until bubbly, about 5 minutes.

Cook's Notes:

If using bacon instead of cooked turkey bacon, saute with the onion in step 1.

You can use gluten-free flour or cornstarch for a thicker soup (about 1 table spoon dissolved in a small amount of water or 1/4 cup cold chicken stock), but this would not be keto friendly.

Nutrition Facts

Per Serving: 347 calories; 25.6 g fat; 13.4 g carbohydrates; 17.7 g protein; 80 mg cholesterol; 1181 mg sodium. Full nutrition

Turkish Eggs (Cilbir)

Ingredients

2 servings

616 cals

For the Yogurt Spread: 1 cup Greek yogurt, at room temperature 1 clove garlic 1/4 teaspoon salt, or to taste 1/2 teaspoon freshly ground black pepper 1 pinch cayenne pepper 2 1/2 tablespoons finely chopped fresh dill, or to taste For the Aleppo Butter: 1/2 stick unsalted butter 1/4 teaspoon ground cumin 1/2 teaspoon smoked paprika 1 tablespoon Aleppo chili flakes For the Optional Parsley and Jalapeno Oil: 1 tablespoon chopped fresh parsley 1 tablespoon diced jalapeno pepper 1 pinch salt (optional) 2 tablespoons olive oil (optional) For the Rest: 1 tablespoon white vinegar, or as needed 4 large eggs 1 pinch sea salt Add all ingredients to list

Directions

Spoon yogurt into a medium bowl. Grate in garlic and mix to combine. Season with salt, pepper, and cayenne. Add dill and mix thoroughly. Set aside at room temperature.

Melt butter in a saucepan over medium heat; heat until bubbles begin to burst. Add cumin, paprika, and chili flakes. Stir until color is uniform, then turn off heat and let spices infuse.

Grind parsley and jalapeno together in a mortar. Season with salt, drizzle in olive oil, and stir to combine.

Fill a large saucepan with 2 to 3 inches of water and bring to a boil. Reduce heat to medium-low, pour in vinegar, and keep the water at a gentle simmer. Crack an egg into a small bowl then gently slip egg into the simmering water, holding the bowl just above the surface of water. Repeat with the remaining eggs. Cook eggs until the whites are firm and the yolks have thickened but are not hard, 2 1/2 to 3 minutes. Remove the eggs from the water with a slotted spoon, dab on a kitchen towel to remove excess water, and place onto a warm plate.

Dollop yogurt mixture onto serving plates. Use the back of a spoon to spread yogurt out into a bed for the eggs, carving ridges into the top to catch the oil. Drizzle on some jalapeno oil. Top with eggs and a spoonful or two of the Aleppo butter. Sprinkle sea salt on top.

Chef's Note:

You can use any other chili flakes in place of the Aleppo variety and, of course, use Turkish yogurt if available.

Nutrition Facts

Per Serving: 616 calories; 57.1 g fat; 8.6 g carbohydrates; 19.9 g protein; 455 mg cholesterol; 743 mg sodium. Full nutrition

Oven-Baked Bacon

Servings: 6

Ingredients

1 (16 ounce) package bacon

Directions

Step 1

Preheat the oven to 350 degrees F (175 degrees C). Line a baking sheet with parchment paper.

Step 2

Place bacon slices one next to the other on the prepared baking sheet.

Step 3

Bake in the preheated oven for 15 to 20 minutes. Remove from oven. Flip bacon slices with kitchen tongs and return to oven. Bake until crispy, 15 to 20 minutes more. Thinner slices will need less time, about 20 minutes total. Drain on a plate lined with paper towels.

Cook's Notes:

If you are making a lot of bacon, the bacon slices can slightly overlap, as the bacon will shrink when baking.

Pour the bacon grease into a jar and allow to cool. Store in the fridge and use instead of oil.

Nutrition Facts

Per Serving:

134 calories; 10.4 g total fat; 27 mg cholesterol; 574 mg sodium. 0.4 g carbohydrates; 9.2 g protein; Full Nutrition

One-Pan Keto Shrimp and Asparagus

Recipe Summary

Prep: 15 mins

Cook: 10 mins

Total: 25 mins , Servings: 1

Ingredients

1 table spoon avocado oil

2 table spoons butter

2 tea spoons minced garlic

¾ pound large shrimp, peeled and deveined

salt to taste

½ tea spoon of red pepper flakes

½ bunch fresh asparagus, trimmed

ground black pepper to taste

1 medium lemon, halved

¼ cup finely shredded Parmesan cheese

Directions

Step 1

Heat avocado oil and butter together in a skillet over medium heat. Add garlic and cook until lightly browned, 1 to 3 minutes. Place shrimp into one side of the pan; season with salt and red pepper flakes. Add asparagus to the other side of the pan and season with salt and black pepper. Flip shrimp after about 2 minutes and roll asparagus over. Squeeze lemon juice on top of shrimp and continue cooking about 3 minutes more. Gently sprinkle Parmesan cheese over shrimp. Transfer to a plate and pour pan juices over shrimp.

Nutrition Facts

Per Serving:

757 calories; 46.5 g total fat; 595 mg cholesterol; 1227 mg sodium. 23.7 g carbohydrates; 70.2 g protein; Full Nutrition

Low-Carb Cauliflower-Spinach Side Dish

Servings: 2

Ingredients

2 ¾ cups cauliflower florets, broken into bite size pieces

2 cups of spinach leaves

2 table spoons butter

1 tea spoon of sea salt

2 spreadable cheese wedges (such as The Laughing Cow® Creamy Swiss Garlic & Herb)

Directions

Step 1

Run cauliflower through a food processor to get 2 cups of cauliflower grounds a bit larger than the consistency of grits.

Step 2

Combine cauliflower, spinach, butter, and salt in a large pot over low heat. Cover and cook until cauliflower is soft and spinach has wilted, 5 to 7 minutes. Stir in cheese wedges until the cauliflower and spinach are coated and no cheese clumps remain.

Nutrition Facts

Per Serving:

180 calories; 14 g total fat; 38 mg cholesterol; 1300 mg sodium. 9.1 g carbohydrates; 7.4 g protein; Full Nutrition

Made in the USA
Columbia, SC
31 October 2023

CONCLUSION

A growing number of studies have been done on the KDE and modified Atkins Diet in adults with seizure disorders, and the results are similar to studies with children. One 2014 study reported that 45% of adolescent and adult participants saw a reduction of seizure frequency of 50% or greater. Tolerability appeared better in those with symptomatic generalized epilepsy.

Interestingly, it was more difficult to keep adults on the diet, since they obviously have more control over what they eat. Research is still limited in this area and more trials are needed.

A 2017 report on use of these diets during pregnancy suggests they may be an effective way to control seizures and could possibly allow pregnant women to use lower doses of epilepsy medication. However, the safety of this still needs to be examined.

Because a high-fat diet runs counter to general beliefs about healthy eating, you may face criticism for putting your child on it. These critics are generally well-meaning, but uninformed. In the end, it's up to you and your child's medical team to determine the best course of action when it comes to safeguarding your child's health.